KU-014-079

WALKABOUT
Changing Seasons

Henry Pluckrose

W
FRANKLIN WATTS
LONDON•SYDNEY

The cold months of winter
have gone.
It is spring.

Cha sons

Leisure & Community Services

last copy (3) 21.

Please return this item by the last date stamped below, to the library from which it was borrowed.

Renewals
You may renew any item twice (for 3 weeks) by telephone or post, providing it is not required by another reader. *Please quote the number stated below.*

Overdue charges
Please see library notices for the current rate of charges for overdue items. Overdue charges are not made on junior books unless borrowed on adult tickets.

WITHDRAWN FROM BROMLEY LIBRARIES

Postage
Both adult and junior borrowers must pay any postage on overdue notices.

-1 MAR 2004	1 4 MAY 2009	
24 JUN 2004		
18 OCT 2004		
2 8 JAN 2006		
1 0 AUG 2006		
19 OCT 2006		
-8 NOV 2006		
2 2 SEP 2007		

**Renewals
0333 370 4700**
arena.yourlondonlibrary.net/
web/bromley

739.96

Bromley
THE LONDON BOROUGH

BURNT ASH LIBRARY
020 8460 3405

BROMLEY LIBRARIES

3 0128 02204 6414

This edition 2003

Franklin Watts
96 Leonard Street
London EC2A 4XD

Franklin Watts Australia
45-51 Huntley Street
Alexandria
NSW 2015

Copyright © 1993 Franklin Watts
Editor: Ambreen Husain
Design: Volume One

All rights reserved. No part of this publication may be
reproduced, stored in a retrieval system, or transmitted
in any form or by any means, electronic, mechanical,
photocopy, recording or otherwise, without the prior
written permission of the copyright owner.

A CIP catalogue record for this book is available from
the British Library.
Dewey Decimal Classification Number: 574.5

ISBN: 0 7496 5268 3

Printed in Hong Kong/China

Photographs: Heather Angel 6, 12, 17 inset, 31;
Bruce Coleman Ltd (E Crichton) 18, (P Clement)
21, (H Reinhard) 23; Eye Ubiquitous (P Prestidge) 4,
(Skjold) 30; Chris Fairclough Colour Library 20, 24;
Robert Harding 7; Frank Lane Picture Agency
(R Wilmshurst) 11, (E & D Hosking) 17, (H Clark)
29; George McCarthy 10; NHPA (S Dalton) 12
inset, (M Grey) 16, (G I Bernard) 18 inset; Oxford
Scientific Films (J Hallet) 8, (A Ramage) 9,
(B Milne/Animals Animals) 28 inset; Swift Picture
Library 28, (M King) 5; ZEFA cover, 13, 14, 15, 19,
22, 25, 26, 27.

BROMLEY PUBLIC LIBRARIES	
02204641	
PET	01-Dec-03
J574 508.2	£4.99
BAS.JPB	

What are the signs of spring?
Trees bud and break into leaf.
The sun is higher in the sky.
It does not get dark so early.
The days grow warmer and longer.

Gardens and parks are bright with spring flowers.

Soon, trees are in blossom.

Animals which have rested
through the winter
become active again.
The hedgehog
leaves its winter home
to hunt for food.

Frogs and toads
find water
in which to lay their eggs.

Most birds build nests
to hold their eggs.
The parent birds sit
on the eggs to keep them warm
until they hatch.

When the eggs hatch
the baby birds have to be fed.

Finding food in spring
and early summer
is much easier than in winter.

Slowly spring becomes summer.
The sun is high in the sky.
The days are longer and
there is more sunshine.
Often the weather is hot
and dry.

Colourful summer flowers
come into bloom.
Trees are full of leaves

and fruit grows fat and juicy
where blossom grew before.

Young animals and birds
leave their nests.
They learn how to find food,
how to climb,
swim
and fly.

Wheat and barley
ripen in the fields.
Summer fruits
are ready to be picked.

As summer ends,
farmers harvest their crops.

Slowly summer becomes autumn.
The days become shorter
and nights are longer.
The sun is lower in the sky.
Cooler weather comes
and many birds fly away
to spend our winter
in warmer countries.

Squirrels, mice and voles
busily gather food
to store away
and use through the winter.

Farmers prepare the fields
for the next crop
in the year which is to come.

Apples and pears are picked and stored...
if they do not get eaten first!

The leaves of many trees start to turn red, orange, yellow and brown.

Birds and small animals feast on autumn berries. Juicy blackberries grow on thorny brambles.

Frost sparkles on leaves and
branches.
The sun gives little warmth.
Many trees are bare.
It is winter.

Very little grows in winter.
Seeds lie in the cold ground,
waiting for the warmth
of the coming spring.
But the cold does not stop
all flowers from growing...
snowdrops push their way up
even through snow.

It is difficult for animals and birds to find enough food in winter.

Some animals go to sleep.
The dormouse finds a warm
sheltered place to spend
the winter.

A heavy fall of snow
makes everything
look different.
If we wear warm clothes
snow and ice can be fun!

Slowly the seasons change.
Winter is turning into spring.
Plants begin to push up
through the earth.
Animals begin to stir.
Once more it is spring.

About this book

Young children acquire much information in an incidental,
almost random fashion. Indeed, they learn much just by being
alive! The books in this series complement the way in which
young children learn. Through photographs and a simple text
the readers are encouraged to comment on the world in
which they live.

To the young child, life is new and almost everything in the
world is of interest. But interest alone is not enough. If a child
is to grow intellectually this interest has to be harnessed and
extended. This book adopts a well tried and successful
method of achieving this end. By focusing upon a particular
topic, it invites the reader firstly to look and then to question.
The words and photographs provide a starting point for
discussion. Discussion also involves listening. The adult who
listens to the young reader's observations will quickly realise
that children have a very real concern for the environmental
issues that confront us all.

Children enjoy having information books read to them just as
much as stories and poetry. The younger child may ignore
the written words ... pictures play an important part in
learning, particularly if they encourage talk and visual
discrimination.

Henry Pluckrose